# KSIHKEHE ALUWOQ
# The LOST SEAL

Words by **Diane McKnight**

Illustrations by **Dorothy Emerling**

Taylor Walkomike tkeyu, kispahte, naka tkolamson walkomike Antarctica. Tamahc, apsokihqon posson pette pemskutek naka milahkukot ponapsqol, nit sipuhsis tolicuwon nit posson qospem pemsokhasol kpoton.

Taylor Valley is a cold, dry, and windy valley in Antarctica. Here, small glaciers reach into fields of bare gray sand and strangely shaped rocks, with streams flowing from the glaciers to frozen lakes on the valley floor.

Taylor Walkomike kci Antarctic Kataskomiq, liwisu McMurdo Walkomike, nit Transantarctic Ktotonuk. Posson eluwe puskonomon Ktotonuk, naka qonahke, Cipenuk Antarctic Posson coceppu Skiyahsonuk Antarctic Posson.

Taylor Valley is one of many valleys in a great Antarctic desert, now called the McMurdo Dry Valleys, located in the Transantarctic Mountains. These mountains are almost buried by ice, and stretch across the continent, separating the East Antarctic Ice Sheet from the West Antarctic Ice Sheet.

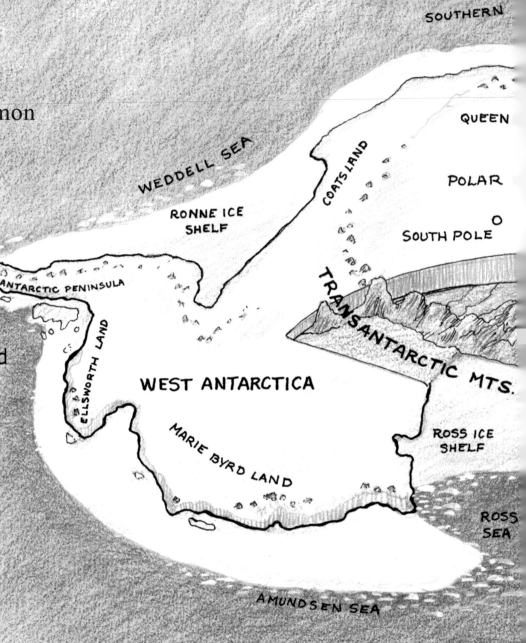

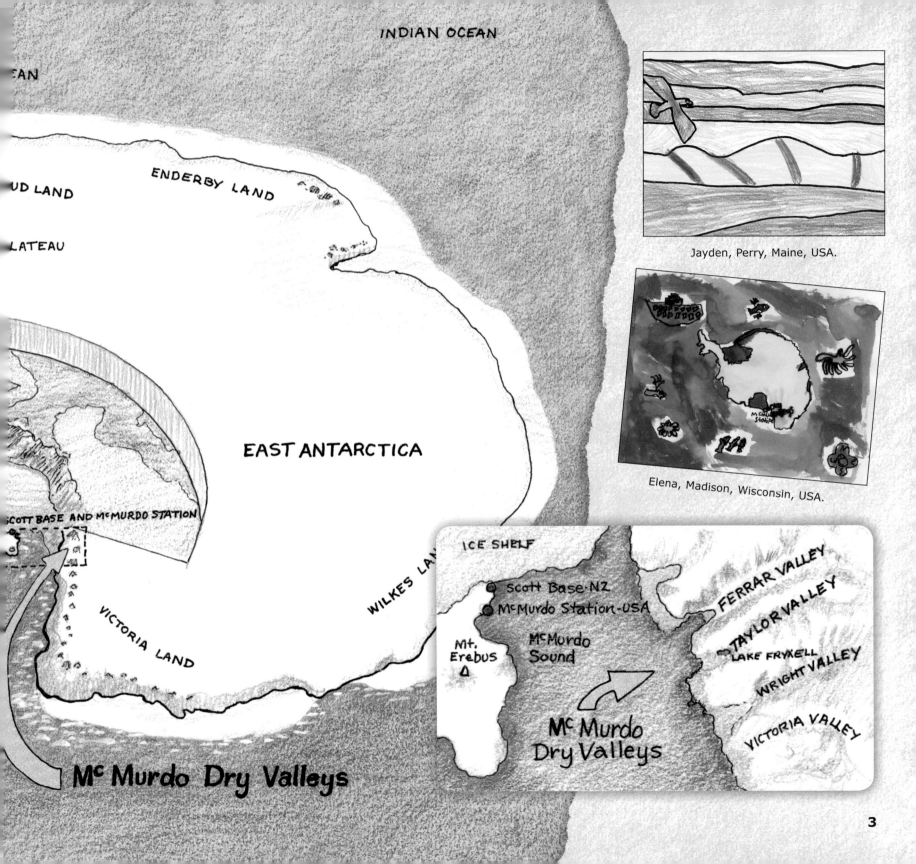

INDIAN OCEAN

ENDERBY LAND

UD LAND

LATEAU

EAST ANTARCTICA

WILKES LAND

SCOTT BASE AND McMURDO STATION

VICTORIA LAND

McMurdo Dry Valleys

Jayden, Perry, Maine, USA.

Elena, Madison, Wisconsin, USA.

ICE SHELF

Scott Base - NZ

McMurdo Station - USA

Mt. Erebus

McMurdo Sound

McMurdo Dry Valleys

FERRAR VALLEY

TAYLOR VALLEY

Lake Fryxell

WRIGHT VALLEY

VICTORIA VALLEY

In 1903, Keptin Lapot Scott naka nisonal wolluhka 'pettehkuwal walkomike apc apacuhsewis Ross Monihq. Keptin Lapot Scott naka nisonal wolluhka 'poneqewolal wesuwew tepiw 'tapakon 'tehsahqehtun posson naka olomapasuwok walkomike.

Keptin Lapot Scott naka nisonal wolluhka moskuwal mummified ahkiq. On kahk-olu kci-katapomic. Wikhikonakonimsu Keptin Lapot Scott papehtokehkikemu qonahke naka liwisu "Kihkanewiw Walkomike."

In 1903, explorer Captain Robert Scott and two members of his Discovery expedition came upon the valley while on their way back to their camp on Ross Island. They left their gear and supplies in a sledge on the glacier and hiked into the valley.

They found no signs of life, only the mummified body of a seal. How it came to be there was a great mystery. In his journal, Captain Scott described the unusual landscape as the "valley of the dead."

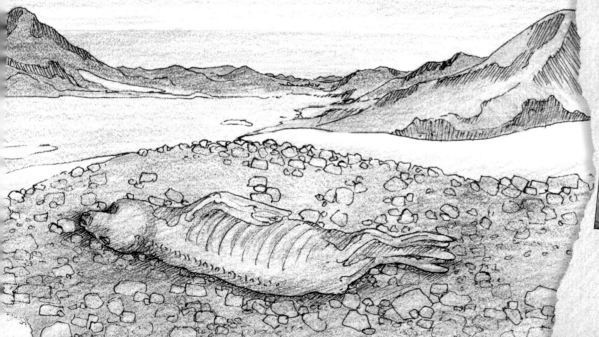

Soonhyun, Madison, Wisconsin, USA.

Alkira, Leongatha, Victoria, Australia.

Katie, Columbus, Ohio, USA.

Keptin Scott 'kisi-iywal katama moskomuwan tepiw sipkawsuwakon woli-niwamke walkomike. Katasu tepiw ponapsqkul naka possonok apsokihqon pematuwet. Nemq ote wewinaqot apsinaqot pematuwet naka wewinaqot esi microscope.

Pemkiskahk, Keptin Scott's wikuwamsis nomihtasu tepiw Wikuwamsis Qonasqamk skitte Ross Monihq. McMurdo Steson naka Scott Wahkaluson wecuwawte. Yat-te Nipon, ktanaqi scientists peciye wikuwamke wot McMurdo woli-niwamke walkomike. Uci scientists 'pawatomon nostomekhal wewskutun sipkawsuwakon sqawsu qocomiw wisoki-tkeyu McMurdo woli-niwamke walkomike.

McMurdo Station

Captain Scott didn't notice the life in the Dry Valleys because he didn't know where to look. Tiny organisms can be hidden by ice and rocks. Some are so small they can only be seen using a microscope. Today, Captain Scott's hut can still be seen on Hut Point on Ross Island. McMurdo Station and Scott Base are nearby. Every summer, many scientists come to the McMurdo Dry Valleys. Some scientists want to understand how life survives in such a cold, hostile environment as the McMurdo Dry Valleys.

Anessa, Boulder, Colorado, USA.

Carolina, Puntas Arenas, Chile.

Scott Base

7

Ktanaqi scientists witoluhkamal lamiw Woli-niwamke Walkomike 't-assokitahaml tolamilke ahkiq. Keptin Scott cu-al-lu qsihtasu Weddell ahkiq hokewey naka Crabeater ahkiq hokewey. Nisiw pskasu lamiw Taylor Walkomike. Nisiw pisessu ewepi walkomike 'tapekte wikuwak kehs mayelok olomiw skitte posson naka mehcinewiw pihce.

Tayen, a scientist winpatokehkimsu elomakomek naka sipuhsisol, 'tatkuhkatomon kotuwitpot kisonuhkot esqonatek kehsanku esqonahtek kehsinsk. Spotew, tepiw Punamuwi, Tayen naka nekom wolluhka sipuhsisol scientists pskasu aqamtek piltuwiku. Ahkiq pskasu tolawsuwiw!

Many scientists working in the Dry Valleys still wonder about the mummified seals. Captain Scott must have seen one of the mummified bodies of Weddell and Crabeater seals now commonly found in Taylor Valley. These seals crawled up the valley from their home miles away on the sea ice and died some time ago.

Diane, a scientist who studies lake and streams, likes to tell the true story about an amazing event that happened in 1990. On a clear, cold, sunny day in late December, Diane and her team of stream scientists found much more than they ever expected. They found a seal—and it was alive!

The scientists 'kekkom Woli-niwamke Walkomike apsokihqon pematuwet. Tepiw sipuhsisol coqolahsiyan, naka moci-wahantuhsis milahkukot pipuwahqot nekosunok. Piskahtetuk woli-niwamke pomamkiye, coqolahsiyan naka moci-wahantuhsis toliku skitte pqiyamkisossis. Apsinaqot naka wakcuwakiye cocuhsok, liwisu nemotodes sqawsu kuwiw naka minuwawsu tayuwek kispastasu. Tehsahqiw posson, coqolahsiyan naka moci-wahantuhsis toliku tepiw apsinaqot lontoq pitsonakon, wisuwonhasu cryoconite alokul. Psahkoniw, neqoloqessu, cahcahqesol naka coqolahsiyan milahkukot tupqancihte, piqosq nekosunok wissekopolikon tomkomike. The scientists munsatahatomon apsokihqon pematuwet. Assokitahsultuwok moskomon tolawsuwiw ahkiq. Tetpomtu mawi-punasu pqonessokhikon skitte sitom naka moskomon putep!

The scientists had come to the Dry Valleys to study microscopic life. In the streams algae, and bacteria form thin mats. In the dark sandy soils, they grow on the sand grains. Small curly worms, called nematodes live in a dormant state and revive only when there is a little moisture. Even on the glaciers, algae and bacteria grow in small pockets of water, called cryoconite holes. On the bottom of the lakes, hidden below the ice, mosses and algae form brown, spongy mats that cover every surface. They were so used to thinking about microscopic life that finding a live seal was as startling as if they had gone to the beach to collect seashells and discovered a whale stranded in the sand!

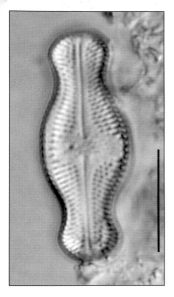

Diatom — *Luticola gaussii*

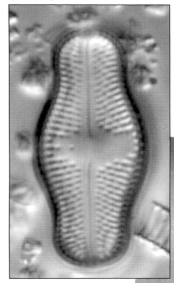

Diatom — *Luticola muticopsis*

Haley, Columbus, Ohio, USA.

Cryoconite hole

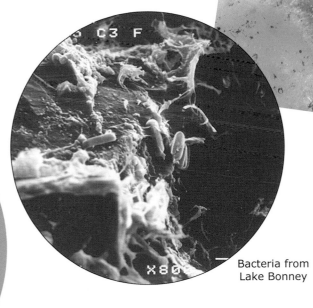

Bacteria from Lake Bonney

Nematode — *Scottnema*

Adam, Buckingham, Pennsylvania, USA.

Pihce yaq iyuwok, the scientists maqenasu samaqan tepiw Tokamonuhk Sispuhsis naka mihqapotomon miyawaptun tepiw wast naka wewinomon pomacqiye tkiqomomqot ptoqap naka tolapekiye esuwiw. Nama wetaptaq pskasu!

A few days earlier, the scientists had been collecting water samples from Canada Stream and had noticed a trail in the snow that looked as if it had been made by someone dragging a heavy bag and swinging it from side to side. There were no footprints!

Jayla, Perry, Maine, USA.

Kenya, Perry, Maine, USA.

Victoria, Perry, Maine, USA.

13

Temonu, Dan, kemp nutahqet, kci-wewis naka nuhsuwaphomon latokiyetul esi pesqon spalikte naka atte. Ehtahkahte, Dan moskuwal ahkiq. Not apaciyewiw peciye kemp naka wolluhkak wisayu qocomiw 'toqiyapotomon. Psi-te wen koskimiye, kahk wolluhkak mulamuwomomqot tucitahasu. Ahkiq mehsihpit wast kolonomuwewsu samaqan naka not 'siwankeyuwal. Ksuhtaqot sehsolamu.

Ksuhtaqot musa milsomal. Tpolutomuwin liwisu Antarctic Conservation Act ankeyutuwakon psi-te kotunkewey of Antarctica maceptuwatomon pomawsuwinuwey utomihkomon. Scientists winpatokehkimsu ahkiq miluwemok kinuwiw 'kiseltomuwal. Apc, psi-te wen apaciye kemp naka telihpumhomuwal the scientists wena winpatokehkimsu ahkiq tepiw McMurdo Sound mihkuluwemal.

Gabby, Perry, Maine, USA.

Thomas, Perry, Maine, USA.

Several days later, Dan, the camp cook, was so curious he followed the unusual trail as it zigged and zagged from one patch of snow to another. Then, Dan found the seal. He came back to camp and the rest of the team rushed out to see for themselves. Everyone was excited, but they also felt a little sad. The seal was eating snow to get water and he looked tired. They knew he must be hungry.

They also knew that they should not feed him. A law called the Antarctic Conservation Act protects all the animals of Antarctica from human interference. Scientists who study seals are given special permits. So, they returned to camp and called the scientists who were studying the seals in McMurdo Sound for advice.

Amanda, Pacifica, California, USA.

15

Mesq-ote Woli-Niwamke Walkomike, kotunkewey wiku tepiw McMurdo Sound. The scientists wena 't-oqimuhtuwal winpatokehkimsu the Weddell naka Crabeater ahkiqok wena komoku naka saputesson posson psikapskiye kotuwihpu etqehom nomehs neqiw. Ciksotaqsit naka Adelie penguins komoku esqayik posson naka kolhike nomehs naka 'kotuwikonal wasisok tepiw kinahantukihqon mawiw tepiw sonuci Ross Monihq.

Psuwis ahkiqok kotunke ahkiqqe naka penguins. Soqskessu tepiw nipon, nehpahtikewin putepiyik macaha Sound naka kotunke.

Emperor Penguin

Adelie Penguin

Unlike the Dry Valleys, many animals live in McMurdo Sound. The scientists they called were studying the Weddell and Crabeater seals that dive through cracks in the sea ice to feed on fish swimming below. Emperor and Adelie penguins dive from the ice edge to go fishing and raise their chicks in large colonies on the coast of Ross Island.

The seals and penguins are hunted by leopard seals. When the sea ice breaks up in the summer, killer whales come to the Sound to hunt.

Thomas, Perry, Maine, USA.

Killer Whale

Leopard Seal

Sepawonuk, nihi ahkiq scientists 'peci-wiciyemal kemp naka wewinomon ahkiq naka wewinomon cokoptihike montokehtasu. Ksihkehewiw ahkiq 'qocikotone wenicanket Weddell ahkiq neketehtuk montokehtasu wot olomussis. The scientists nulomi-nsotuhmon olomahtu wot wenicanket ahkiqok olomi-nawtaqot naka kiluwahsu naciptun wiku. The scientists wolitpihike pomtokot, wihqonomuwewan 'pokahkonihtehmon, naka suncokhikon sqoccihte amalekok naka nacihtun nokomasitahatomon moskomuwan ahkiq ehtahkahte nipon.

The next day, three seal scientists came to the camp and identified the seal from the flipper tag on his tail flipper. The lost seal was a one-year-old male Weddell seal that had been tagged when he was a pup. The scientists explained that it is a natural behavior for young male seals to wander away looking for a new home. They measured exactly how long he was, took a sample of his blood, and painted an orange stripe down his back to make it easier to find the seal the next summer.

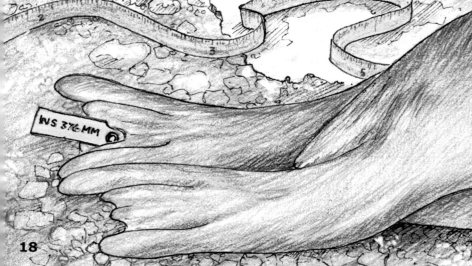

Tamata, Pleasant Point, Maine, USA.

Lindsey, Eastport, Maine, USA.

Kara, Perry, Maine, USA.

1

Ahkiq scientists wewi ahkiq kat-op sqawsu puniw. Piskahtetuk, tkopekot naka minus newinsk degrees Celsius. Ksolamson, liwisu Katapomic wocawson, puniw tollamson Cipenuk Arctic Posson, tollamson 'qotatq cel newinsk awa.

Amkis kiwtahqiyamu mulahkecuwon ponapsq naka supeyu. Kekesk

ventifacts piluwahkukot tallamson naka wewinomon ocisok naka tuwihputiyil naka ehtuwopiyamkil, pili-mawe-punasu tomkomike Antarctic micuwakoninut.

The seal scientists knew that the seal would not survive the winter. When the sun does not rise, it can get, as cold as -40 °C. Strong winds, called katabatic winds, rush down in the winter from the East Antarctic Ice Sheet, blowing as fast as 140 miles per hour.

The wind-blown sand wears down the rocks and makes them smooth. Some of these ventifacts are shaped by the wind to look like large pieces of cheese or tables and benches, creating a fine place for an Antarctic picnic.

Kira, Perry, Maine, USA.

Lindsey, Eastport, Maine, USA.

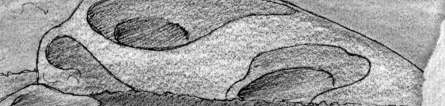

21

Kotoki-sepawonuk ahkiq scientists apacuhsewiw McMurdo Sound, sipuhsis scientists natoluhke. 'Qoci-nipon, kisuhs kat-op apc nasokahte naka 't-oqetpekonomuwan neqiye psanakiw, uloposomon tepel posson 'qasqomaqosomon. Anqoc kse-tkeyu posson samaqan posson wisayu naka cipokalokinaqot nahkaw sipuhsis naka kompe tepiw elomakomek, kahk anqoc sipuhsisol tolopehtehson. Spotew wolapon, 'sukanomon naka tkiqokimqot wolitpihike milihtasu.

After the seal scientists returned to McMurdo Sound, the stream scientists had to get back to work. In summer, the sun never sets and the average temperature is just below freezing, warm enough for the glacier ice to be melted by the sun. Sometimes the cold meltwater from the glaciers comes rushing and roaring down the stream channels and floods into the lakes, but sometimes the streams are only trickles of water. Because it was a sunny day, streamflow was high and there were important measurements to be made.

Jorjah, Orange, New South Wales, Australia.

Kate, Boulder, Colorado, USA.

Megan, Columbus, Ohio, USA.

Harrison, Orange, New South Wales, Australia.

Nucikhahsit wolluhka tepiw Woli-niwamke Walkomike 'sotuwa ahkiq askuhpal 'qotuhkapu naka olomiyewiw, kahk scientists mulamuwomomqot nikiwomolsu naka assokinahsu eyik ahkiq.

Nisukonokkiwiw, a helicopter sakom wewiye ahkiq 'peci-wiciyemal kemp, 'topolutomon pahpuwe ahkiq wolahqe ocis wiyuhsol pasqihihqu! Psi-te wen assokinaqot naka wewi kemp nama wiku siktelamu ahkiq. The scientists 'telihpumhomuwal McMurdo Steson apca. 'Kisolutomon 'siki ksihkehewiw ahkiq skituwiw supeq posson-ahkiq weceyawit wiku.

The research team in the Dry Valleys understood that the seal should be left to go his own way, but they felt uneasy and wondered where he was.

Two days later, a helicopter crew chief discovered that the lost seal had come to the camp, joking that the seal must have smelled their cheeseburger dinner! Everyone was astonished and knew the camp was not a proper home for a lost, starving seal. They called McMurdo Station again. A decision was reached to bring the lost seal back to the sea ice—his natural home.

Marion, Whiting, Maine, USA.

Jayden, Perry, Maine, USA.

Ella, Perry, Maine, USA.

The Helicopter mawapasuwok sakom
'poneqewolal 'teponahqalal ap
wecuwawtehkomon ahkiq nacihtun
haystins tutonahsu. Wisokokihqon
psiksoq 'tehsahqi-punomon ap naka
wissekhasu 'somakonoss polahkitol.
The scientists mawkuwa ahkiq 'sitoqomutun
'somakonoss polahkitol, naka skihkipolahsut ahkiq.

Kskikon sqoccihte nutiyapekustun naka wiwonatokehtun
mettokopu, liwisu pendant, siciw apcituwiye
supeqahkomiq toloka tehsahqiw. The helicopter
't-amihkomon haystins naka ahkiq nipaphal New Harbor!
Apcituwiye woleyutomuwakon ahkiq! Nucituwiyat
'punomuwewal haystins tutonahsu nahkaw
wecuwawtehkomon Weddell ahkiqok naka
nahnaktehsin the helicopter wecuwawte.
Ksihkehe ahkiq 'sikte-koti-nomihtun
naka naciptun skitte posson nekom-ote
woniyakon nihkankomon saputesson ap,
eluwe cihpolopilsu.

The helicopter crew chief put down a cargo net near the seal to make a sling load. A large piece of plywood was placed on the net and covered with Army blankets. They herded the seal onto the blankets, and strapped him down.

A wide orange rope with a loop at the end, called a pendant, was attached to the bottom of the helicopter that hovered overhead. The helicopter lifted up the sling load and the seal was off to New Harbor! The flight must have been quite a ride for the seal! The pilot set the sling load down near some other Weddell seals and landed the helicopter nearby. The lost seal was so eager to get onto the sea ice that he pushed his head forward through the net, almost tangling himself in a knot.

Gustavo, Puntas Arenas, Chile.

Alonso, Puntas Arenas, Chile.

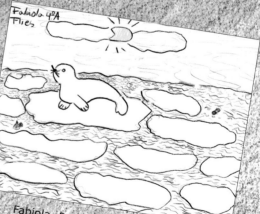

Fabiola 4°A
Flies

Fabiola, Puntas Arenas, Chile.

On kahk-olu 'siyehlal! Ahkiq 'sasotomuwan wast. The Helicopter olomamu, wolluhka amante ksihkehe ahkiq mosonomuwewal nomehs neqiw posson, katok tolikhahsu kemp ocis wiyuhsol.

Temonuk, Tayen's wolluhka kisolutasu macewiyal sihpusisol winpatokehkimsu. Wisuwonhomon wicuhketomon 'teyphomon wolitpihike pihtuwahte tepiw steson.

28

Finally he was free! The seal started eating snow as fast as he could. As the helicopter took off, the team hoped that the lost seal would soon be catching fish under the sea ice, rather than looking for cheeseburgers back at the camp.

Later on, Diane's team decided to name the streams they were studying. Having a name would help them keep track of all the measurements made by the instruments at each gauging station.

Gizem, Madison, Wisconsin, USA.

Tolicuwon naka 'teyphomon kehs samaqan tepiw elomakomek 'qoci-nipon. 5,000 naka 10,000 wolitpihike 'teyphomon yat-te sipuhsisol 'qoci-nipon naka qoci wolitpihike mawwikhomon. Tpaskuwakon wisuwonhomon tomkomike Antarctica. Liwihtasuwiw etoli tomkomike, naka 'pehqiyal wenaw mawoluhke tomkomike, naka ktonukot eleyik kisitpiye asitiw. Tayen's wolluhka wisuwonhomon pesqon sipusis tolicuwon tepiw Elmakomek Fryxell; Ksihkehe Ahkiq Sipuhsis.

Ksihkehe Ahkiq ktonukot tomk 'teyphomon mihkuhsatomon pomawsuwinuwok naka tolawsuwiw ahkiq tepiw Woli-Niwamke Walkomike. Pemkiskahk psi-te wen 'kisuwehkan map moskomuwan Ksihkehe Ahkiq Sipusis naka 'pisuwi-nomihtun miliye ksihkehe ahkiq.

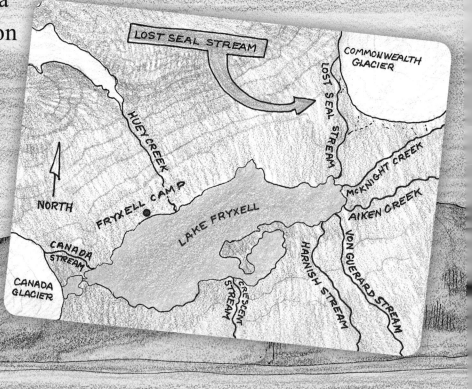

By knowing the flow rate, it is possible to know how much water is flowing into the lake each summer. For each stream about 5,000 to 10,000 measurements are recorded every summer and then all of these measurements are added up.

There are rules for naming places in Antarctica. Names can describe a particular place, or can be chosen to honor people who have worked there, or to commemorate an event that happened there. Diane's team chose to name one stream that flows into Lake Fryxell; Lost Seal Stream. This name celebrates the first recorded encounter of humans and a live seal in the Dry Valleys. Today anyone can use their map to find Lost Seal Stream and imagine the adventure of the lost seal.

Chelsea, Leongatha, Victoria, Australia.

Amy, Arbury, Cambridge, England.

# The LOST SEAL

Published by Taylor Trade Publishing

An imprint of The Rowman & Littlefield Publishing Group, Inc.

4501 Forbes Boulevard, Suite 200, Lanham, Maryland 20706

www.rowman.com

Unit A, Whitacre Mews, 26-34 Stannary Street, London SE11 4AB

Distributed by NATIONAL BOOK NETWORK

Library of Congress Cataloging-in-Publication Data Available

International Standard Book Number:
ISBN: 978-163076-255-1

The paper used in this publication meets the minimum requirements of American National Standard for Information Sciences—Permanence of Paper for Printed Library Materials, ANSI/NISO Z39.48-1992.

Printed in the United States of America

To my husband Larry and our daughters
Rhea and Ariel.
—DM

To Paul for his steadfast support.
—DE

## Acknowledgements

*Thanks to the following schools for their participation in this project:*

- Arbury Primary School, Carton Way, Cambridge, UK
- Beatrice Rafferty School, Pleasant Point (Sipayik), ME, USA
- Belle Valley School, Erie, PA, USA
- Bixby School, Boulder, CO, USA
- Bluffsview Elementary School, Columbus, OH, USA
- Buckingham Elementary School, Buckingham, PA, USA
- Corbridge Middle School, Northumberland, UK
- Creative Environment Day School, Fayetteville, NY, USA
- Escuela Jose Manuel Balmaceda, Recreo, Chile
- Flossmoor Montessori School, Flossmoor, IL, USA
- Granby Elementary School, Columbus, OH, USA
- The German School of Puntas Arenas, Puntas Arenas, Chile
- Kapanui School, Waikanae, Christchurch, New Zealand
- King's Highway Elementary School, Clearwater, FL, USA
- Kinross Wolaroi Preparatory School, Orange, NSW, Australia
- Lanikai Elementary School, Kailua, Hawaii, USA
- Lee St. Primary School, Carlton North, Victoria, Australia
- Leongatha Primary School, Victoria, Australia
- Liberty Elementary School, Columbus, OH, USA
- Margate Primary School, Tasmania, Australia
- New South Wales Primary School, Yarramundi, NSW, Australia
- Ocean Shore School, Pacifica, CA, USA
- Qinnguata Atuarfia School, Kangerlussuaq, Greenland
- South Hornby School, Hornby, Christchurch, New Zealand
- Shorewood Elementary School, Madison, WI, USA
- Tarras School, Central Otago, New Zealand
- Winner Education, Cangshan, Fuzhou, China

This material is based upon work supported by the National Science Foundation under grant no. DEB1346857. Any opinions, findings, and conclusions or recommendations expressed in this material are those of the author and do not necessarily reflect the views of the National Science Foundation.

## About the Long Term Ecological Research (LTER) Network (lternet.edu)

The LTER network is a large-scale program supported by the National Science Foundation. It consists of 25 ecological research projects, each of which is focused on a different ecosystem. The goals of the LTER network are:

**UNDERSTANDING:** To understand a diverse array of ecosystems at multiple spatial and temporal scales.

**SYNTHESIS:** To create general knowledge through long-term interdisciplinary research, synthesis of information, and development of theory.

**INFORMATION:** To inform the LTER and broader scientific community by creating well-designed and -documented databases.

**LEGACIES:** To create a legacy of well-designed and -documented long-term observations, experiments, and archives of samples and specimens for future generations.

**EDUCATION:** To promote training, teaching, and learning about long-term ecological research and the Earth's ecosystems, and to educate a new generation of scientists.

**OUTREACH:** To reach out to the broader scientific community, natural resource managers, policymakers, and the general public by providing decision support, information, recommendations, and the knowledge and capability to address complex environmental challenges.